Fevered Imaginings & Disparate Dreams

I0416274

A Collection of Erotica

By

Jeff Longren

Preface

Herein you will find flights of romantic fancy, and hardcore action to get you started. The most erotic organ is the one between your ears, I just hope to inspire a few of you readers to step a little outside of your own expectations and join me through the looking glass, in some cases the darker side, in others the lightness of being in love. Which is which, I leave you to decide.

------Jeff Longren

Summer Storm

It began as a whisper, a gentle caress and the question

"Are you ready for this?" Tracing the lines of her face with

fingertips calloused by experience and weather.

He had never needed to raise the level of His voice for her to

hear him, the undulation of tone sent shivers along her spine.

She nods her head in assent.

"Do you want the blindfold, or do you want to see your admiring

audience?"

Again her wordless yea, and He steps behind her to place the

black velvet over her eyes. With a gentle tug, she is led to the

cross, dependent on him for sight and direction, trusting literally

blindly in this man, this man, to honor her submission to Him.

With care He guides her hands into the cuffs she enjoys so

much, now fastened to spring loaded links at the head and foot

of the cross, her temporary prison. No matter how she may

stretch and contort, she is secured against the unforgiving

structure, safe and at calm.

He has made Himself familiar with the rhythm of her body, and

uses those same gentle hands to cup her buttocks first in one

and then the other, gripping and pulling her towards him. It

makes her feel uniquely feminine, as if He was steadying

Himself to thrust deeply into her. With each caress, insistent

and then teasing, she arches into Him driven by her desires.

*You never told me how to begin, your preference. The rope or

the leather?* His voice is amused, as if either choice would lead

to shock and surprise. At her whispered decision, His hands

leave her body, and she is plunged into anticipation. Where the

first stroke might fall, how deeply it might bite. She has chosen

the leather, for all that it was thinner and more of a sting, and the

knotted ends of the rope gave her pause.

"The House safe-word is Red, and there is no shame in

speaking it. *This is new for you, this situation and the bite of*

My instrument."

The first strokes are as a gentle rain, almost a whisper along her

back and torso exposed and vulnerable to His efforts. With a

moment more, the summer rain increases in intensity to a volley,

the tips of the leather biting in random patterns across her back

and thighs. Each time her gasps arise in pitch to what He

judges is the edge of her comfort, the rain stops, and His hands

are back, lovingly cupping and rubbing away the burn of the

leather.

"Do you want the rope instead? you are doing so well, I am

proud of your effort. Everyone watching sees how beautifully

you strain against the cuffs, how pretty you are when you twist

to avoid the sting."

The rope has knots, it's true, but the weight is heavier. Like the

storms that she has seen out her window the first falls are large

6

and round, building in volume until the whole of her back sings

with ongoing sensation, saturated with the thicker bite of the

knotted nylon. As before, He drops the intensity and tends to

her when the flood threatens to overwhelm her, like the

unexpected shelter of a tree cradling her from the onslaught.

In time, her knees start to buckle and her legs turn to jell. Too

soon, she inwardly cringes at how far she has to go for her flesh

to last long enough to release the endorphins she craves. He

unshackles her, holding her upright against Him as her arms fall

to her sides. Settling her head in his chest, she asks for a couch.

Fall of Rain

She walks slowly into the dance club, her fine black hair pulled back from her porcelain features with a white band to keep the expected evidence of her exertions from marring her makeup. She wants to dance, fitting her way in the throng as carefully as she chose her outfit hours before. Clad in a turquoise and sea-green t-shirt dress baring a white shoulder, her legs cased in sheer black leggings, she is uncertain, trembling, and eager to surrender to the throb of the music in her ears and the steady pull of lust in her veins. Her toes curl in the new 4 and ½ inch black heels bought for occasions like this as the throng of people around her press against her budding breasts (so sensitive) and hands brush against her rounded ass barely covered by the dress. It is a validation, this anonymous attention, for all that it is strange it thrills her to feel the evidence that her efforts are not unseen, that her flesh is molding itself to her will.

She moves to the bar, pulling liquid courage from the bartender as assuredly as she bolsters her self-confidence from the pressed bodies against her own. She had often considered herself an exhibitionist, and this unknown appreciation of her charms has combined with the gin to propel her to the crowded dance floor.

But what good is dance without a partner? She scans the single patrons, hoping for someone that meets her dreamlike image of masculinity so long as he does not speak and ruin the illusion for her. From behind her a light tap on her shoulder, and warm breath husking into her ear.

"Would you like to dance with me?"

The voice is deep, with an edge of roughness in it that lights the banked embers of her desires. She half turns, all that is possible in the crowded entrance to the dance floor, to look up into clear blue eyes framed behind gold rimmed glasses, set in a lightly bearded face with lips that quirked in a half-smile as he looked her over in the strobes flickering. He stood easily above her, his broad shoulders, wide chest and long athletic arms making her feel even more delicate, more like a drop of dew than a woman. Her nod had him drawing her close to him and resolutely pulling her into the wave of dancers, his hand closing around her own like a promise of safety, the light squeeze at her fingertips hinting at more.

The newly minted couple reached the edge of the floor by virtue of his bearing. Watching him as he made his way deftly through dancers, muddled conversation and observers was like watching a carefully choreographed battle. For all his size, he moved surgically through the crowd, never hurried but not stopping until his goal was reached. She thrilled, wondering if his girth and grace would translate to a firm lead, a hand cradling her hip and his eyes locked on hers.

Her musing came to an end as he swept her into a primitive rhythm, his own feet barely moving as he matched his hips to hers without effort, his hands resting casually along her waist as if guiding her into this dance. She looked down to keep her heels from crushing his toes, and thrilled anew when she realized her partner wore not only a light blue polo that echoed his vision, but a kilt that ended just above his knees. Calves like piano wire pulled taut and painted a light tan, dusted with hair led into black combat boots as he moved his hips to roll into her own with the beat of the music.

As her eyes traveled the length of his frame, they met his own, a twinkle of amusement showing. Quickly she slipped back a pace, turning around so she could evade the open disarming frankness of his gaze, laying bare her desire as if party to it. She backed up to feel his muscular thighs pressed tight against her own, and gasped, the sound lost in the sea of passions around her as she felt his palms rest first lightly against her thighs, then more insistently as he drove himself closer to her with the beat of the music. He was aroused, and she felt the thick head of it creeping across the edge of her buttocks as she ground into him. Though her eyes were closed, and she faced away from her momentary lover, the sheer magnetism of his presence echoed in her senses as she fitted her hips against his waist and let the songs transport her away from care, enjoying the throbbing beat settled between her legs.

She had become adept at gauging a man's size through this method, and delighted to find him just thick enough to rest inside the cleft of her ass, yet long enough to slip the head between her legs to where she might catch a glimpse if she looked down.

For the space of a quarter hour she drifted, letting the sounds pounding in her ears match the thrill of the man so near to her as to be inside her save the flimsy material of their clothing. He was skilled, taking the beat to drift his muscular legs down the length of her own before edging against her in a lull, as if by accident. She no longer cared, her head keeping time as her hips pushed back on his shaft, her mouth opening in wordless sighs when his hands trailed from hip to breast and down again. Her exposed flesh caught fire when his fingers grazed it, and her breath felt hot when she felt his at the nape of her neck. The music ended, people started moving around her, no longer caught in the beat and perhaps their own fantasies. She turned to thank him, hoping to hear the bass rumble that had so captivated her earlier, only to catch a flash of his black kilt whipping in the sudden void around them. As quickly as he had appeared, he as gone, the scent of cigar tobacco and sandalwood in his wake.

Heart of Winter

She mouthed the words, her thin lips accentuated by carefully applied dark liner and ruby red paint. Her body sheathed in an evening dress tight enough to lay bare her curves, and inspire fresh imaginings of what lay under the frills and furls of fabric. She had chosen the dress to go with the song so carefully, and her popularity showed the time she spent on her performances.

So she sang along with a woman she had never met, the words echoing in her heart as her lips pursed and she held her hands aloft; "I will lay my hands down and surrender...". Too often the words of this song played and she watched lovers walking hand in hand in the club, singing the words to each other in hushed voices. Too often her fans sang these words to her, as if they could brush aside the curtain and hold her close enough to chase away the demons of her past.

She finished the song to thunderous applause, but her mind

was on the cool drink waiting for her backstage. Since this was her

last number, though, she must stay front and center, lend her

enthusiasm and support to her fellow chanteuse. Taking in the

crowd, a few couples, a bridal party, the usual collection of drunk

and rowdy college boys that while fun to look at, shied away from

doing anything other than a furtive grope under the garish lights of

the stage so they could brag to their friends later. She looked long

and hard at the man seated alone, away from the lights. His face

was in shadow, but she could make out broad shoulders cradling a

head crowned with thick brown hair. His face was hidden, but there

was a glint of glasses in the reflected stage lights, and the jaw was

covered in a mat of fur the same russet brown as the locks of his

head. The pool of shadow he sat in did not quite conceal firm legs

left bare and likewise hairy, ending in leather sandals reminiscent of

roman gladiators.

16

She stood, as part of her duties included feeling out potential tippers from the throng of enthusiastic revelers. Striding easily in her 3 inch heels, taking care not to snag the train of the dress on the corners of tables between her and her prey, she was in front of him, fanning herself from the heat of both the lights and the humidity. It must have been obvious that she was feeling the 90 degree evening, because her quarry produced a white handkerchief from a pouch at his waist, offering it to her.

She smiled her thanks, also sitting alongside him when he patted the seat. As she eased in, his arm rested across the tufted back of the seat, near enough to snuggle in if she wanted, but far enough away not to cause offense.

They spent the next hour this way, her murmured comments about other performers met with a smile or a bent head when he could not hear over the music. When the lights came up, she mentioned she had to change and hoped to see him outside so they could continue the conversation, perhaps somewhere quieter. His easy grin and casual touch to her shoulder communicated more than enough his desires.

As she changed from the evening dress into a miniskirt with a neckline that plunged just north of her navel, something significantly shorter and more suited to seduction than conversation, she talked to another performer about him. He was quiet, kind, and quick to laughter. His questions were not pointed nor upsetting, rather they were probing and she felt as if he filed all of her answers away for recall in seconds when needed. Many say that women decide in 5 minutes or less whether they will sleep with someone; she took a bit longer but the offer to join her at home was a foregone conclusion when he kept his eyes on her own rather than her chest as they spoke.

She had asked for a gap of perhaps 15 minutes to ready

herself before he joined her. She used the time to adjust her

makeup, change into her favorite slip dress, and sip at a soda. He

texted from the driveway, and she replied that the door was open, as

was she.

He met her at the top of the stairs, wrapping an arm around

her waist with assertive actions and reaching a hand behind the base

of her neck to caress the short hairs curling there. As he ascended,

his lips covered over her collarbone, than her neck, leaving feather

light tastes of her punctuated by his beard until his lips were

hovering over her own. He paused, just breathing in the scent of

her, inhaling on her exhalations, absorbing her with as many of his

senses as possible. His eyes drank in her face, cheekbones high,

now pale lips poised in a cupid's bow, eyes astonished. His hands

traced circles over her back, cupping her ass lightly before roving over the muscles of her shoulders. He leaned into her, listening to her increasingly rapid heartbeat. His nostrils flared, more surely drunk on her recently cleansed scent than the few drinks he had imbibed. His lips finally brushed her own, the tongue trailing ever so gently over each lip before pulling them into his own, savoring the tight pucker and feeling them soften to his ministrations.

Her hands were likewise busy, curled around his powerful shoulders and draping over the corded weight of them. She trailed a hand down towards his ass, expecting to find whatever shorts he had worn to expose his muscled legs, only to slip aside the back of a kilt and rest on the fine pelt of hair covering his rear. As she kneaded the flesh, it pulled taut in her fingers, making the muscles stand out in sharp relief. She moaned at the awareness of his scent, his flesh molded to her own so forcefully, and the scent of him filling her nostrils as she surrendered to the carnal tide rising within her.

She pulled him into her, backing up to the nearest couch in her apartment and dropping to pull at the front of the kilt. With a tug he was freed in the air conditioning, then quickly enveloped in the hot moist confines of her mouth. She enjoyed feeling him swell within her, and if she didn't act quickly that moment would be lost. He breathed in sharply, his right hand curling around the base of her hair as she flicked her tongue. She had started her adventures this way, and still enjoyed the sense of power that controlling a man with her skills brought her.

Too soon he pulled himself away, she looked up meeting his eyes as he led her up the stairs to her four poster oak canopy bed. She had carelessly discarded earlier wardrobe choices, and these he moved to the side as he laid her down gently on the bed with a gleam in his eyes.

She trembled, feeling his hands at the juncture of thigh and hip, insistently pulling her legs apart and then holding her down. With a soft cry, she welcomed first the shadow of his beard, then the softness of his lips along the large vein in her groin, then the wetness of his tongue along the recently bare flesh of her sex. The shock was all at once too much, her back arched, her ass ground into the bed beneath her, and she shuddered from the onslaught of her first orgasm that night.

A Spring in her Step

She walked into the room, her auburn hair cascading around high cheekbones framed by the rounded lenses of her glasses, the only concession she made to her age. While many of the patrons of this place were her contemporaries, many more were not. She sought out the back where a group was huddled on a queen sized bed, catching sight of a distinctly masculine shape near buried under the ministrations of two other women. Nude to her gaze, he seemed somehow aloof from the woman with her legs astride his own, the other dropping kisses along the rider's upturned face.

She came here as an escape, her life not allowing for anything more than the most casual of interludes. The men here were avid in their attentions, the women sated easily from the steady parade of flesh walking in all states of dress and undress. Her quarry was momentarily forgotten as she was greeted by a warm set of lips meeting her own in a passionate greeting. She adored the feel, taste and intimacy of kissing, so much so it was required for her to become aroused.

The brunette commanding her attention slipped aside, her immediate assault upon the lush lips of our beauty halted by the single mindedness of her pursuit. She had an ache inside her, one that the man lying underneath two women already could fill with the thrust of his hips.

Her lips pursed as she looked steadily at him, eying the thick cock rising from his muscular thighs with a practiced glance. Firm, the shaft tapering ever so slightly beneath the glans, which ended in a flare just wide enough to ease her desire but not cause her discomfort. She approved of the curled hairs around the base, the sac lying beneath them trim but not shaved free of down. Men ought to be hairy, near bestial in their appearance, all the better to ride them into submission under her own thighs, slaking her own

thirsts.

Sliding a hand around the base of him, she flicked her

tongue along the sensitive corona and watched his reaction. While

he smiled, her efforts were met more with a pleasant regard than the

shudder she was accustomed to. He smiled a bit wider, exposing

firm even teeth in a face framed with the edges of a goatee, "Where

you have your fingers is more sensitive than there, sweet." So she

would need to swallow this man to arouse his passions? All well and

good, she gripped behind the shaft and cupped the silky balls,

rolling them gently in her fingers, stroking the skin between the base

and his rear. His eyes rolled back at that, she smiled. Opening her

mouth carefully, she dropped her head alongside his flesh, not

closing her lips until she had buried it as deeply as she could within

her first line of offense.

A sharp intake fixed her eyes back from the rise and fall of

his stomach to his face. He had not lied about his preference, his

eyes were wide and his lips trembled as she lathered his cock in her

saliva. Flicking her tongue along the vein writ now large and thick in

her mouth, she gradually reversed direction until only the tip was

inside her, then throated him in a single motion, burying her nostrils

into the patch of hair along the base of her lust object. She was

pleased to smell a faint aroma of soap, perhaps a hint of cologne,

but nothing overpowering. She repeated this motion twice more,

bathing his cock in as much of her saliva as she could, gesturing

frantically to the other now watching women to assist in opening a

condom

This was a critical moment. So long as his attention was on

her mouth and the heat of it, slipping the protection over him and

then him as deeply inside her as she could manage would be fluid, easy, and seamless. Should his attention wander, the thick pulsing

hardness in her mouth would not continue to fill her, stretching her,

keeping her connected to her own femininity. She had lost more

promising men than this one to the sudden departure of her mouth

being replaced by the impersonal grip of latex, and she had learned

adept ways of managing the trick.

Keeping him soaked with her saliva, she allowed her friends

to remove her own clothing, her shirt having been freed before she

bent to her task, (her full breasts capped with aureoles wide as her

thumb never failed to capture attention) and attend to her own

lubrication. Fingers splayed her, slid the length of her as they made

certain she was ready to mount the man before her. With enough

lubricant, anything is possible, regardless of her own distractions.

As she stroked and licked the flesh before her, her other

hand warmed the condom to approximate her body heat, unrolling it and clutching it in her fingers right before she slipped the now

sodden head of his mast inside the form fitting prophylactic. Easing

it down the shaft was simple at this point, as she fit the suddenly

wider cap of him to herself expectantly.

The Brush of Silks

She walked in, surveying the room in front of her with careful trepidation. She ran her blue lacquered fingertips along the short black skirt she wore, feeling the tops of her stockings secure thereunder the edge. With a shake of her fine brown hair, she looked to one of the men she trusted to do such things for her, to her. He indicated the head of the bed, motioning where she ought to put her arms and legs for ease of movement.

Before she set to, she faced him, a thrill playing over her finely boned features. Full lips pursed, her tongue flicking out to wet suddenly dry areas as he lifted the swath of black felt to be doubled around her eyes. The blindfold was necessary, as it freed her to react and not feel self conscious about how she looked to others.

She let herself be led to the surface of the bed, her waist

cradled by pillows set to maximize her rear peeking under from her

skirt. Legs splayed, arms spread apart, all of her extremities were

bound in soft cuffs with an inner core of steel. From experience she

knew she could pull on them to her heart's content, and would, and

they would not yield.

A hand caressed her ass, and she squirmed, only feeling the

sensation, not knowing if it was one of the men or the other. Eager

for this to begin, she arched herself into the probing hand, rough

from callouses and playing with the seam at the edge of her legs and

thighs.

A loud crack entered the room, as his hand (their hands?

She felt two distinct patterns of stroking before the first blow fell)

bounced off of her with a sudden flurry of strikes. Her back arched,

driving her face deeper into the cushion of the bed and her ass higher into the oncoming strikes. As much as she tried to move away

from this, she craved it, the knowledge that nothing she did would

allow her escape save a spoken word agreed upon beforehand.

The hands echoed their assault, pausing when she fell

exhausted against the restraints, stroking and kneading the flesh to

keep the blood close to the surface. She thrilled to the

disembodied sensations, the sting as a different tool was used to

raise the tingling and the thud as a heavier object was brought into

play. Thrashing around on the bed, her sweat pooling under her

makeshift blindfold, she understood both that her struggles were

useless and fueled the rain of blows upon her rapidly warming flesh.

Panting with the exertions, she sagged against the ropes

pressing her into the bed, knowing the pictures taken now would

only remind her of this moment. Bright lights immortalizing the

creeping flush to her ass, the glistening sheen of her own work to avoid and encourage. She felt her sex swell with the attention, the

multiple hands moving over her flesh, and she opened her mouth to

voice not a moan, not a yelp, but a request;

"I want both of you, I need both of you inside me."

She felt her legs parted as she asked, the sure evidence of

their arousal hot against her leg and cheek. With a wave of her hand

she dismissed removing the cuffs at her wrists and ankles; the sex

was hotter with the hint of resistance. She plunged her mouth over

one of her men, tasting the root of him in a quick swallow as the other

plied her sex with fingers and wet, preparing her for the thrust. She

felt hands at the small of her waist, steadied herself on the hips of

the man before her as she flicked her tongue to his appreciative

moans and whispered encouragement. This was the heart of who

she was, how she wanted to be, a tool used by the men to fulfill their

desires, an empty vessel being filled fore and aft by their lusts. This is who she was right now, and it felt glorious to have one man sawing

at her insides with first gentle thrusts, then steady rhythm until she

was arching her back to meet him. If she chose to, she could identify

this lover by his manner alone; the gentle giant, the caring

considerate monster that she had asked to arrange her restraint and

subsequent spanking. His hands wrapped around her buttocks

comfortably, slapping them easily with each thrust deep into her

being, mixing the savagery of his hands with the tender pressure of

his cock.

Or this man, his cock in her mouth, his hands at her head,

pushing her to accept more of his length down her throat. Forceful,

using his free hand to caress her sides and breasts, this man was the

shorter, more hesitant of the two. Eager to explore this with her,

but needing the steady hand of the man inside her to the hilt to

watch over them both.

She moaned around the mouthful she had, pushing herself against the thick invasion of her body. This was fantasy too, one that might or might not end with a bang. She traced the veins of the cock in her mouth, tasting the sweet tang of him, regretting that wisdom and prudence meant she could only feel the pulsing inside her to show if her efforts to milk the other bore fruit. To and fore they plumbed the depths of her, the seesawing motion setting her own pulse to quickening.

With a cry she took the one from her mouth and shuddered, the tide breaking over her in waves, burying her face in the waist of the man before her, drinking in the scent of him as her gentler lover eased his assault. She lie there, her body twitching as each muscle knotted and every nerve sang its own song of triumph and joy.

Postlude

Each of these stories is about a trans woman. Pre-operative, non-operative, and post-operative, every tale reflects possible emotions, thoughts, desires and interludes for them. The author has found lovers, friends and partners among them, and laid these stories to paper in order to show how close to the surface each woman is, how truly universal desire and passion can be.

Support the LGBT community, and act locally, thinking globally.

Be well